Fast,
Pray,
Give

Making
the
Most
of
Lent

a six-week guide

Franciscan
MEDIA
Cincinnati, Ohio

Cover and book design by Mark Sullivan
Cover image © iStockphoto | Ekely

LIBRARY OF CONGRESS CATALOGING-IN-PUBLICATION DATA
Fast, pray, give : making the most of Lent : a six-week guide.
p. cm.
Includes bibliographical references and index.
ISBN 978-1-61636-538-7 (alk. paper)
1. Lent—Miscellanea. 2. Spiritual life—Catholic Church. 3. Christian life—Catholic authors. 4. Catholic Church—Doctrines.
BV85.F37 2012
263'.92—dc23
2012034039

ISBN 978-1-61636-538-7

Published by Franciscan Media
28 W. Liberty St.
Cincinnati, OH 45202
www.AmericanCatholic.org
www.FranciscanMedia.org

Printed in the United States of America.
Printed on acid-free paper.
12 13 14 15 16 5 4 3 2 1

| CONTENTS |

Introduction

Beware of practicing your piety before others in order to be seen by them; for then you have no reward from your Father in heaven.

Whenever you give alms, do not sound a trumpet before you, as the hypocrites do in the synagogues and in the streets…. But when you give alms, do not let your left hand know what your right hand is doing, so that your alms may be done in secret; and your Father who sees in secret will reward you.

And whenever you pray, do not be like the hypocrites; for they love to stand and pray in the synagogues and at the street corners…go into your room and shut the door and pray to your Father who is in secret; and your Father who sees in secret will reward you.

And whenever you fast, do not look dismal, like the hypocrites, for they disfigure their faces so as to show others that they are fasting…put oil on your head and wash your face, so that your fasting may be seen not by others but by your Father who is in secret; and your Father who sees in secret will reward you.

—Matthew 6:1–8, 16–18

Catechism Quote

The New Law *practices the acts of religion:* almsgiving, prayer and fasting, directing them to the "Father who sees in secret," in contrast with the desire to "be seen by men." Its prayer is the Our Father.[1]

—CCC, 1969

Fast, Pray, Give: Making the Most of Lent is designed to help you learn more about the customs and practices of Lent, as well as the Catholic teaching behind these. It is about growing spiritually during Lent, especially through using the traditional Lenten practices of fasting, prayer, and almsgiving. But we'll take those practices one step further in this book: Instead of focusing simply on their traditional meaning, we'll give each of them a fresh perspective by placing them in the context of simplicity, spirituality, and stewardship. These latter three disciplines are important to the life of Catholics today, and are essential components of an engaged faith.

• **Simplicity** calls us to focus more on what we need, and less on what we want. It is doing without the excesses of modern life, and living in accordance with Jesus's words in Luke 14:33: "So therefore, none of you can become my disciple if you do not give up all your possessions."

• **Spirituality** is the way we live out our faith. It shapes our lifestyle and determines our ways of prayer, as well as how we worship God.

• **Stewardship** is the free gift of our time, talent, and treasure. It is how we use our God-given talents and abilities in Christian service to one another.

Each chapter in *Fast, Pray, Give* opens with a Scripture passage from the Gospel for that Sunday in Lent; the Third, Fourth, and Fifth Sundays use the Year A readings, in keeping with the RCIA. A quote from the *Catechism of the Catholic Church* is next, giving context from Church teaching to what is presented in the chapter. Next you'll find background material on the topic for that week, followed by two questions for reflection and discussion to help better bring the subject matter into your own life. The section titled "Inspiration From the Saints" offers further fruit for contemplation, while the Practice and Prayer sections give you inspiration to go out into the world with what you have learned in that particular chapter.

Fast, Pray, Give uses as its foundation content from *Catholic Update* newsletters. The main section of each of the chapters is adapted from a particular *Update* that you'll find noted at the end of that section. The section "Inspiration From the Saints" is taken from "Saints: Holy and Human," *Catholic Update*, by Michael D. Guinan, while the "Practice" comes from *Wondrous Encounters: Scripture for Lent,* by Richard Rohr. All of these *Updates*—and many more that deal with topics pertinent to Lent —are available from Franciscan Media and can further enhance your Lenten prayer and practice.

Finally, there is a companion DVD available for use with this book. It offers additional information on Lent and brief commentaries on the Year A Gospels that can be used with this six-week study guide, especially in conjunction with the RCIA.

There is more information in the Leader's Guide on how to use the DVD with this book.

May this joyful season of Lent bring you to a deeper understanding of your faith, and a richer practice of its Lenten customs and traditions. By following in the footsteps of Jesus Christ and the teaching of the Church, let us join together to become stronger disciples and a faith-filled people who can negotiate through the Lenten desert into the Easter light of Resurrection.

What Is Lent?

Then Jesus was led up by the Spirit into the wilderness to be tempted by the devil. He fasted forty days and forty nights, and afterwards he was famished. The tempter came and said to him, "If you are the Son of God, command these stones to become loaves of bread." But he answered, "It is written,

'One does not live by bread alone,
   but by every word that comes from the mouth of
   God....'"

Again, the devil took him to a very high mountain and showed him all the kingdoms of the world and their splendor; and he said to him, "All these I will give you, if you will fall down and worship me." Jesus said to him,

"Away with you, Satan! for it is written,
'Worship the Lord your God,
   and serve only him.'"

Then the devil left him, and suddenly angels came and
waited on him.

—Matthew 4:1–4, 8–11

Catechism Quote

Jesus' call to conversion and penance, like that of the prophets
before him, does not aim first at outward works, "sackcloth and
ashes," fasting and mortification, but at the *conversion of the
heart, interior conversion.* Without this, such penances remain
sterile and false; however, interior conversion urges expression
in visible signs, gestures and works of penance.[2]

—CCC, 1430

How is the emphasis on conversion and penance found in this
quote from the *Catechism* different or the same from your
understanding of Lent?

_____

_____

_____

_____

It All Starts With Baptism

Since the Second Vatican Council, the Church has reemphasized the baptismal character of Lent, especially through the restoration of the catechumenate and its Lenten rituals. Our challenge is to renew our understanding of this important season of the Church year and see how we can integrate our personal practices into this renewed perspective.

Lent as a forty-day season developed in the fourth century from three merging sources. The first was the ancient paschal fast that began as a two-day observance before Easter but was gradually lengthened to forty days. The second was the catechumenate as a process of preparation for baptism, including an intense period of preparation for the sacraments of initiation to be celebrated at Easter.

The third was the order of penitents, which was modeled on the catechumenate and sought a second conversion for those who had fallen back into serious sin after baptism. As the catechumens (candidates for baptism) entered their final period of preparation for baptism, the penitents and the rest of the community accompanied them on their journey and prepared to renew their baptismal vows at Easter.

Prior to Vatican II, Lent was all about self-denial, suffering, and the death of Christ in bloody agony on the cross. When the council issued the Constitution on the Sacred Liturgy in 1963, the bishops called for the renewal of the season of Lent:

> The season of Lent has a twofold character: primarily by recalling or preparing for baptism and by penance, it disposes the faithful, who more diligently hear the word of God and devote themselves to prayer, to celebrate the paschal mystery. This twofold character is to be brought into greater prominence.... Hence, more use is to be made of the baptismal features proper to the Lenten liturgy....[3]

The council's reference to the baptismal character of Lent seemed strange to many people at the time, who had not been trained to link baptism and Lent in their minds or in their devotional practices. Yet Lent is fundamentally baptismal in its origins and its meaning.

Prayer, Fasting, and Almsgiving

The three traditional pillars of Lenten observance are prayer, fasting, and almsgiving.

Prayer during Lent should draw us closer to God. We might pray especially for the grace to live out our baptismal promises more fully. We might pray for the elect who will be baptized at Easter and support their conversion journey by our prayer. We might pray for all those who will celebrate the sacrament of reconciliation during Lent that they will be truly renewed in their baptismal commitment.

Fasting is one of the most ancient practices linked to Lent. The early Church fasted intensely for two days before the celebration of the Easter Vigil. This fast was later extended and became a forty-day period of fasting leading up to Easter. Vatican II called us to renew the observance of the ancient paschal fast: "…let the paschal fast be kept sacred. Let it be celebrated everywhere on Good Friday and, where possible, prolonged throughout Holy Saturday, so that the joys of the Sunday of the Resurrection may be attained with uplifted and clear mind."[4]

Almsgiving is a sign of our care for those in need and an expression of gratitude for all God has given to us. Works of charity and the promotion of justice are integral elements of the Christian way of life we began when we were baptized.

In Lent, we are asked by the Church to celebrate the sacrament of penance, because Lent is the season for baptismal preparation and renewal. Those who experience the loving mercy of God in the sacrament of reconciliation should find themselves standing alongside the newly baptized at Easter filled with great joy at the new life God has given all of us.

Lent comes to an end before the evening Mass of the Lord's Supper on Holy Thursday. That liturgy begins the Triduum, the great three days that celebrate the central mystery of our faith.

(Adapted from Rev. Lawrence E. Mick "Lenten Customs: Baptism Is the Key," *Catholic Update,* March 2003.)

Forty Days of Preparation
During the forty days of Lent, we share with the whole Church an annual "wilderness experience." The questions and issues we face are basically the same as those faced by the people of God in both the Old and New Testaments.

In many languages—for example, Spanish, *Cuaresma*—the name for the season before Easter is derived from the Latin word for *forty*, a clue that something else important is happening. The forty days of Lent recall the forty days of Jesus's being tempted in the wilderness (Matthew 4:1–11; Mark 1:12–13; Luke 4:1–13), and Jesus's temptations recall the forty years of Israel's temptation in the wilderness on their journey to the Promised Land—among other Old Testament accounts (see Genesis 7:4, 12, 17; 8:6; Exodus 24:18). In the New Testament, not only is Jesus tempted in the desert for forty days and nights, but his ascension to heaven occurs forty days after the Resurrection (Acts 1:3).

Numbers in the Bible are often not meant to be taken literally, but serve a symbolic function. The number forty denotes a period of preparation for some special action of the Lord; it is a time of grace. After the flood in Genesis, a new creation begins. After Moses converses with God, the covenant is renewed. After Israel's wandering in the wilderness, they will enter into the Promised Land. After Jesus's temptation in the desert, he begins his public ministry; after the ascension, we enter the age of the Church.

7

Many spiritual writers speak of a "wilderness experience." This is a kind of retreat experience, time set apart to focus on, to ask, to consider, to respond to basic questions of the spiritual life. Lent is the Church's annual "wilderness experience," its retreat to ask again the basic questions of our faith.

The people of Israel certainly knew the real wilderness, since that would describe fairly well the regions to the south, southwest, and east across the Jordan. The desert is a place of no water and no food since little vegetation can grow there. It is also the abode of dangerous animals. The desert is a place of extremes where choices are more clear-cut.

In the Gospels, Jesus is tempted in the wilderness to be a different kind of Messiah; to take the path of spectacle and power rather than that of humble service, but this temptation would continue throughout his ministry up to his death itself when he is taunted to come down off the cross.

In both the Old and New Testaments, the wilderness symbolizes three main themes:

A Place of Covenant

The main thing that happened to Israel in the wilderness was their covenant with Yahweh at Mount Sinai, which calls them to a whole different view of reality, a new set of values, and a totally different style of life. To live the covenant truly is to worship this God and to be concerned for the rights and needs of others.

During his temptations in the wilderness, Jesus is tempted to live by a set of values totally different from those of the Father. Will he be the kind of Messiah that God was calling him to be, or would he go the more culturally acceptable way of power, prestige, and spectacle? We know the answer.

During Lent we examine our lives in the light of our sharing in the covenant of Christ. We too are called to a view of reality and a set of values quite different from those of the culture(s) around us. Do we really embody them in our lives?

A Place of Testing

The wilderness was also the place where Israel was tested in its faithfulness to Yahweh and where it repeatedly failed. The wilderness is a place of extremes, and choices are more clear-cut. Food and water are essential for physical survival; security from external threat and internal stability are essential for social survival. These are legitimate needs, but in the wilderness, they become temptations for Israel's faith: Will they maintain their faith in the God who brought them safely from Egypt and who guides them in the wilderness? They often failed.

Jesus, in the wilderness, was also tempted about food, but unlike Israel, he kept his faith in God. What of us? As strongly as we may say that we want—and really intend—to follow God, many forces remain, within and without, to pull us away and push us toward idols. It is always the most legitimate needs (e.g., food, water, defense, internal order) which can become the most seductive idols. Is our service of God the true foundation of our life?

A Place of Presence

The wilderness was a place of threats to life and of death. The Israelites are tested to see if, in fact, they will truly believe that their God, a God of life, is with them there.

Jesus never wavered in his close relationship to God. We Christians are assured that Jesus indeed is "God with us" (see Matthew 1:23), and he has assured us, "And behold, I am with you always, until the end of the age" (Matthew 28:20). In the midst of our struggles, temptations, journeys, do we really believe that God is with us? The wilderness is a place to nurture our belief that God is truly with us.

The Bible bears witness that it is all right not to know the details of the future. We do know the most important thing about it: We are not alone; "God is with us!" The words addressed first to Israel speak to us as well: "Do not be afraid, for I am with you" (see Genesis 28:15; Exodus 3:12). Whatever the future brings, we will make it together; we will persevere even through death itself. Lent, after all, looks forward to Easter!

(Adapted from Michael D. Guinan, O.F.M. "In the Desert with Jesus: Biblical Themes of Lent," *Catholic Update,* February 2005.)

Questions for Reflection and Discussion

In his 2005 commencement address at Stanford University, Steve Jobs asked, "If today were the last day of my life, would I want to do what I am about to do today?" What aspect of your daily life could benefit from a focus this Lent on conversion?

_____

_____

_____

_____

One of the prayers said when ashes are given on Ash Wednesday is "Turn away from sin and be faithful to the Gospel." Is there a Gospel practice that you might want to further explore this Lent?

_____

_____

_____

_____

Inspiration From the Saints
Martin de Porres (1579–1639)

Martin was born in Lima, Peru. Son of a Spanish knight and a black former slave woman, he joined the Dominicans as a lay brother and showed great love for the poor. He mixed a life of deep prayer with service in the kitchen and laundry and with giving alms at the front door. Though Martin's dark skin linked him with a minority class, his own care reached out to all human beings regardless of race or social status. He often cared for slaves brought in from Africa. Martin's example of universal love can serve as a model for our Lenten practice.

Martin de Porres is the patron saint of interracial justice and harmony, and inspires the Church to open the ranks of sainthood to a wider ethnic diversity. How can you reach out to people from other backgrounds this Lent?

_____

_____

_____

_____

Practice

In all three years of the lectionary cycle, the Gospel for the first Sunday of Lent is devoted to the temptation of Jesus in the desert. Examining temptations is a good way to begin Lent. Most people's daily ethical choices are not between total good and total evil, but between various shades of good—a partial good wrongly perceived as an absolute good, or even evil disguised as good. These are what get us into trouble.

This week, look at what tempts you most. What can you do this week to work toward changing your response to that temptation?

Prayer

God of all creation, turn my mind and my heart away from what leads me to sin. Create in me a new heart, one that is centered on you alone. Give me the grace to live each day this Lent guided by your great commandment, loving you, my neighbor, and myself with unconditional love. Amen.

Prayer

Six days later, Jesus took with him Peter and James and his brother John and led them up a high mountain, by themselves. And he was transfigured before them, and his face shone like the sun, and his clothes became dazzling white. Suddenly there appeared to them Moses and Elijah, talking with him. Then Peter said to Jesus, "Lord, it is good for us to be here; if you wish, I will make three dwellings here, one for you, one for Moses, and one for Elijah." While he was still speaking, suddenly a bright cloud overshadowed them, and from the cloud a voice said, "This is my Son, the Beloved; with him I am well pleased; listen to him!" When the disciples heard this, they fell to the ground and were overcome by fear. But Jesus came and touched them, saying, "Get up and do not be afraid."… As they were coming down the mountain, Jesus ordered them, "Tell no one about the vision until after the Son of Man has been raised from the dead."

—Matthew 17:1–9

Catechism Quote

God calls man first. Man may forget his Creator or hide far from his face; he may run after idols or accuse the deity of having abandoned him; yet the living and true God tirelessly calls each person to that mysterious encounter known as prayer. In prayer, the faithful God's initiative of love always comes first; our own first step is always a response. As God gradually reveals himself and reveals man to himself, prayer appears as a reciprocal call, a covenant drama. Through words and actions, this drama engages the heart. It unfolds throughout the whole history of salvation.

—CCC, 2567

How is God revealed to you most often? In prayer? At liturgy? In the quiet of a field, or in conversation with a friend?

_____

_____

_____

_____

What Is Prayer?

Prayer is communication with God, the way that we grow and nurture our relationship with the Lord. We pray in thanksgiving, with gratitude for all God has given us. We pray in petition, asking God for what we want or need (Matthew 7:7–8). We pray in adoration, to worship the divine presence. And we pray to confess our sins, to express our sorrow and seek forgiveness.

Any good relationship needs constant communication to stay healthy and vital; so too our relationship with God. There are many ways to pray, and opportunities exist in any part of our day to be open to the spirit of God, ready to hear his voice and respond in kind. How we pray will depend on our spirituality, that is, the way we live out our faith. Let's take a look at what that means.

Today there is a great hunger and thirst for more authentic spiritual life—in short, for spirituality. Look at Christianity, Buddhism, Islam, or any number of religions, and you will find they share the quest of the human spirit for something bigger, deeper, beyond the ordinary experience of life.

Christian spirituality, though, stresses that we begin with the gift from above, from the Holy Spirit of God. You could even define Christian spirituality as "our life in the Spirit of God" or "the art of letting God's Spirit fill us, work in us, guide us." The Holy Spirit makes us holy, calling each of us to be a saint, a holy person. For the Christian, then, *spiritual* refers to the whole of our existence, filled with the Spirit of Christ. We are so filled with this Spirit that Paul can say, "It is no longer I who live, but it is Christ who lives in me" (Galatians 2:20).

Christian spirituality deals with the whole person—body and soul, thoughts and feelings, emotions and passions, hopes, fears, dreams—as we live in and with the power of the Spirit. And it deals with the whole life of the whole person, calling us to live this life to the fullest. The call and challenge of the spiritual life is not restricted only to some Christians (priests or vowed religious, for example) but is addressed to all. All share the same Spirit and are called to one and the same holiness.

At times we hear talk of different spiritualties: Franciscan, Jesuit, lay, priestly, and so on. How can this be if there is only one Christian spirituality? The answer lies in the broad diversity of human experience. All of us belong to particular religious communities into which we are born, in which we grow, are educated, come to know and experience God. These circumstances shape our response to the Spirit's call, and are but different responses to the one common Christian call to holiness.

(Adapted from Michael D. Guinan, O.F.M. "Christian Spirituality: Many Styles—One Spirit," *Catholic Update*, May 1998.)

The Examen of Consciousness

During Lent, we are called to conversion and repentance. A good way of looking at the events, habits, and choices of our day is the Examen of Consciousness, which is part of the Spiritual Exercises of St. Ignatius Loyola (1491–1556).

Ignatius, founder of the Society of Jesus, was a very practical man when it came to prayer. He recommended to his brothers a daily method of examining their lives so that they might better serve the Lord. Ignatius taught that the key to a healthy spirituality was twofold: Find God in all things and constantly work to gain freedom to cooperate with God's will. He proposed a daily exercise, which he called the Examen, that has been used by many Christians ever since.

There are five simple steps to the Examen. Find a quiet place where you will not be disturbed. Perhaps light a candle or change the lighting in the space. Then sit comfortably, as straight-backed as possible with both feet on the floor. Feel God's presence and know his deep love for you; you are about to enter into a deep and intimate conversation with Jesus, your closest friend, ally, and advocate.

1. *Recall you are in the presence of God.* We are always in the presence of God, but in prayer we place ourselves in God's presence in an especially attentive way. God your Creator knows and loves you in the deepest way possible, and through Jesus his Son you have learned of your own beauty. The Holy Spirit, the

manifestation of the love between the Father and the Son, guides and guards us too. Ask the Holy Spirit to help you look at your life with love this day.

2. *Look at your day with gratitude.* After a few moments, begin to give thanks to God for the gifts of this day. Special pleasures will spring to mind: a good night's sleep, the smell of the morning coffee, the laugh of a child. Recall the gifts of your own creation, the special and perfect way God has made you and which brings God's grace to others: your sense of humor, your ability to cook, your strong hands and arms, your words of encouragement, your patience. As you complete the review of your gifts and the particular gifts of this day, pause briefly to thank God for all these.

3. *Ask help from the Holy Spirit.* Ask here in a special way for the Holy Spirit to come into your heart and to help you look at your actions this day clearly and with an understanding of your own limitations. The Spirit will help you understand the mystery of your human heart; ask to learn more about your actions and motivations. Remember, this is not a "beat up on yourself" session, where you grind at the core of your being in sadness

over things you have done wrong. Rather, it is a gentle look with the Lord at how you have responded to God's gifts.

4. *Review your day*. This is the longest of the steps. Here you review your entire day, watching it like a little movie that replays in your mind. Be sure to notice the details, the context of what happened and how you acted. As you look through the day, notice especially your interior motives and feelings. Please don't try to fix everything here. The key to the Examen of Consciousness is to do just that: Examine just how conscious you have been of God's presence and actions in your life.

- When did you fail? Perhaps you were cross with someone, but why? God might prompt you to remember that it is really time to get new shoes! Or God might show you that the person reminds you of a long-lost enemy. Perhaps you were too tired to really work effectively.

- When did you love? One or more of your actions may have been completed in near-perfect freedom. You can recall that you actually were able to choose a specific course that served the common good and the needs of the individual freely, without any "ulterior motive" on your part, in genuine love and charity.

Habits are an especially good thing to notice in the Examen. If your daily habits are dragging down your freedom, in the Examen you will notice them very quickly. Take this opportunity to see where Jesus has helped you to have a positive response to life as well. Maybe you could have accepted more help from Christ in one or another of your events this day, but if you did receive his suggestion then notice that as well.

5. *Reconcile and resolve.* In this final step, have a heart-to-heart talk with Jesus. Imagine Jesus, your trusted friend, sitting right there beside you, or before you. Perhaps he holds your hands in his, and looks into your eyes. Perhaps the two of you sit side by side, a couple of old buddies looking out at the ocean. Here you talk with Jesus about what you did and what you did not do.

Maybe there was something you did wrong—not particularly sinful, but not particularly smart either. Now is the time to tell Jesus you are sorry, and to ask him to be with you the next time the same sort of situation arises. Remember all the good things, and thank the Lord for being with you when you avoided a wrong choice, or when you resisted an old temptation to unfreedom. Feel the sorrow in your heart when you apologize, but also feel the gratitude when you give thanks for God's gentle work inside your heart as he continually labors to make you more Christ-like, day by gentle day.

End the entire Examen with the Our Father.

The graces that you will gain in the Examen of Consciousness, the intuitions of what it is God wishes you to do, will come inside and outside of other regular prayer in addition to this time in the Examen: the Mass, personal meditation, reading of Scripture and of spiritual books. You will continue to grow in God's love, but you will also recognize that you are the hands and heart, the eyes and ears, the very voice of Christ.

(Adapted from Phyllis Zagano, "Examen of Consciousness: Finding God in All Things," *Catholic Update*, March 2003.)

Questions for Reflection and Discussion

Pierre Teilhard de Chardin is often credited with saying, "We are not human beings having a spiritual experience; we are spiritual beings having a human experience." How does your spiritual nature blend with your human nature?

_____

_____

_____

_____

What is your favorite way to pray?

_____

_____

_____

_____

Inspiration From the Saints
Elizabeth Ann Seton (1774–1821)

The first American-born saint (in New York City), Elizabeth Ann Seton married and bore five children. After the death of her husband, she became a Roman Catholic and began to serve the poor in the Baltimore area, especially in the field of education. A well-educated woman, she trained teachers, wrote textbooks, translated spiritual writings from French. Elizabeth Ann founded the Sisters of Charity and is considered a founder of Catholic parochial school education in the United States. At her canonization in 1975, Pope Paul VI praised her for her contributions as wife, mother, widow, and consecrated religious.

Elizabeth Seton's gift to the Church today is her witness to an authentic American spirituality in a land where temporal prosperity threatens to extinguish it. How can your prayer strengthen your courage to witness to the faith?

_____

_____

_____

_____

Practice

In the story of the Transfiguration found in this Sunday's Gospel, the disciples are overwhelmed by God's brilliance. After this awesome and consoling epiphany, there is clear mention of "a cloud that overshadows" everything. We have what appears to be full light, yet there is still darkness. Knowing, yet not knowing. Getting it, and yet not getting it at all. Isn't that the very character of all true mystery and every in-depth encounter?

Open your mind and your heart this week to see God in every person with whom you interact. Look for the spark of the divine in each one.

Prayer

God of all creation, our hearts are restless until they rest in you. Help us to live each day in the footsteps of Jesus, our model in true humility and joy. Let us see you in every person we meet, and in every moment of our day. With the psalmist, we pray, "Search me, O God, and know my heart; test me and know my thoughts" (Psalm 139:23). Amen.

Fasting

So he came to a Samaritan city called Sychar…Jacob's well was there, and Jesus, tired out by his journey, was sitting by the well. It was about noon. A Samaritan woman came to draw water, and Jesus said to her, "Give me a drink."…The Samaritan woman said to him, "How is it that you, a Jew, ask a drink of me, a woman of Samaria?"…Jesus answered her, "If you knew the gift of God, and who it is that is saying to you, 'Give me a drink,' you would have asked him, and he would have given you living water." The woman said to him, "Sir, you have no bucket, and the well is deep. Where do you get that living water?…Jesus said to her, "Everyone who drinks of this water will be thirsty again, but those who drink of the water that I will give them will never be thirsty. The water that I will give will become in them a spring of water gushing up to eternal life." The woman said to him, "Sir, give me this water, so that I may never be thirsty or have to keep coming here to draw water."

—John 4:5–15

Catechism Quote

The precepts of the Church are set in the context of a moral life bound to and nourished by liturgical life. The obligatory character of these positive laws decreed by the pastoral authorities is meant to guarantee to the faithful the very necessary minimum in the spirit of prayer and moral effort, in the growth in love of God and neighbor: ...The fourth precept ("You shall observe the days of fasting and abstinence established by the Church") ensures the times of ascesis and penance which prepare us for the liturgical feasts and help us acquire mastery over our instincts and freedom of heart.[5]

— CCC, 2041, 2043

The word *discipline* derives from the Latin *discipulus*—the same root as the word *disciple*, a pupil or follower. What area of your life can most benefit from discipline at this time?

_____

_____

_____

_____

What Is Fasting?

Fasting is one of the most ancient practices linked to Lent. In fact, the paschal fast predates Lent as we know it. The early Church fasted intensely for two days before the celebration of the Easter Vigil. This fast was later extended and became a forty-day period of fasting leading up to Easter. Vatican II called us to renew the observance of the ancient paschal fast: "let the paschal fast be kept sacred. Let it be celebrated everywhere on Good Friday and, where possible, prolonged throughout Holy Saturday, so that the joys of the Sunday of the Resurrection may be attained with uplifted and clear mind."[6]

Fasting is more than a means of developing self-control. It is often an aid to prayer, as the pangs of hunger remind us of our hunger for God. The first reading on the Friday after Ash Wednesday points out another important dimension of fasting, when the prophet Isaiah insists that fasting without changing our behavior is not pleasing to God:

> Is this not the fast that I choose:
>   to loose the bonds of injustice,
>   to undo the thongs of the yoke,
> to let the oppressed go free,
>   and to break every yoke?
> Is it not to share your bread with the hungry
>   and bring the homeless poor into your house;
> when you see the naked, to cover them,
>   and not to hide yourself from your own kin?
>
> —Isaiah 58:6–7

Fasting should be linked to our concern for those who are forced to fast by their poverty, those who suffer from the injustices of our economic and political structures, those who are in need for any reason. Thus fasting is linked to living out our baptismal promises. By our baptism, we are charged with the responsibility of showing Christ's love to the world, especially to those in need. Fasting can help us realize the suffering that so many people in our world experience every day, and it should lead us to greater efforts to alleviate that suffering.

Catholics between the ages of eighteen and fifty-nine are obliged to fast on Ash Wednesday and Good Friday. In addition, all Catholics fourteen years old and older must abstain from meat on Ash Wednesday, Good Friday, and all the Fridays of Lent.

As explained by the U.S. bishops, fasting means partaking of only one full meal. Some food (not equaling another full meal) is permitted at breakfast and around midday or in the evening—depending on when a person chooses to eat the full meal. Abstinence forbids the use of meat, but not of eggs, milk products, or condiments made of animal fat.

Simplify

During Lent, another way to fast is by making a conscious attempt to simplify our lives.

The lives of Jesus and the saints show us that living simply can be a means of spiritual growth, and there is no doubt that our twenty-first-century culture presents a real challenge to simplifying our lives. Yet there is no better time than Lent for exploring what "faithful simplicity" means in our lives. It is a move away from the things of the world, toward the fullness of the feast found in God's love.

Living complicated, too-busy lives in a consumer-driven culture has not been good for us—as individuals, as families, or as a society, and we Christians are called to live simpler lives as an expression of our faith. Jesus set an example of simple, worry-free living. We're taught that it's a matter of justice not to use more than our fair share of the world's resources.

The thought of cutting back on commitments or clearing out our clutter may be overwhelming. It appears easier to continue doing what we do and hope things will change someday. Worse yet, we're surrounded by temptations to complicate our lives further: ways to better our careers, activities we're asked to do, things we want to buy—including the latest gadgets or books that promise to simplify our lives!

Yet the call to simplicity, to faithfully live the Gospel, is still there. It's all throughout the Scriptures. It's in the teachings of Jesus, the example of the saints, and the exhortations of the Church. This consistent message may seem an indictment of our consumer lifestyle and an attempt to make us feel guilty, yet our hearts really long for a simpler, more basic lifestyle.

Probably the most forceful teaching of Jesus about simplicity is found in the Gospel of Matthew: "Do not worry about your life, what you will eat or what you will drink, or about your body, what you will wear…. Do not worry about tomorrow, for tomorrow will bring worries of its own" (6:25, 34). In ten verses, Jesus covers the whole gamut of the unsimple life: from concerns about food, drink, and clothes to the worry that complicates all our lives.

But how are we to carry out these exhortations not to worry? The answer to that comes later in Matthew's Gospel, in one of the most beloved Scripture passages in the Bible: "Come to me, all you that are weary and are carrying heavy burdens, and I will give you rest. Take my yoke upon you, and learn from me…and you will find rest for your souls. For my yoke is easy, and my burden is light" (11:28–30).

Jesus's life was anything but simple. Sure, he lived in an agricultural society with fewer distractions than we have today. But it wasn't a simple society, nor was Jesus's place in it free of troubles or demands. Requests for his services were unending. His disciples had their own ideas about who he was and agendas about what he should do. The religious leaders first opposed him, then plotted his death.

How did Jesus stay free of worry and faithfully simple? He went off to pray first thing every morning. Jesus understood, Son of God though he is, that we human beings need time to get away from others, to pray and receive strength and courage for the day ahead.

Inner Simplicity

We cannot have outer simplicity in our homes and schedules without inner simplicity. And, if we are at peace inside, if we lean on and learn to trust God for our needs, our outer lives will reflect that.

We can begin to seek this balance from the outside in or from the inside out. If we clean up our outer clutter, we will become less scattered and chaotic inside. The reverse is also true. If we set aside time for God first thing in the morning as Jesus did, we'll find more energy for simplifying our environment. We'll also make better choices about how we spend our time, money, and energy. Here are a few ways to begin.

1. *Keep a simple, fifteen-minute, appointment with God for prayer.* Begin by saying a simple prayer. The Lord's Prayer, said slowly as you think about each line, is a good way to start. Then move on to write in your journal or pray for your needs or the needs of others. End simply by trying to keep still and quieting the chatter in your head. Rest in God's presence and absorb God's love and light.

2. *Chart your time for two days—one weekday and one weekend day.* Include personal hygiene, meal preparation, and time spent with family and friends, paying bills, watching television, reading, and so on. Now put a red check next to those things that sap your energy and a green star next to those things that rev you up, that you enjoy doing. Do you have more red checks or green stars? What could you do to add more green to your life and minimize the red?

3. *Ask a friend to help you clear your clutter, perhaps from a closet or garage.* Then reciprocate by doing the same at your friend's home. It's easier and faster to work with someone else. Another person's objectivity helps us see our possessions in a new light and enables us to part with items we neither need nor want.

4. *Start a stream-of-consciousness journal.* You don't have to be a great writer or good at expressing yourself. Simply write about your problems, relationships that trouble you, the state of your home, or your thoughts about your boss. Writing about your worries is a great life-simplifier. This exercise can help you clarify problems, or it may simply allow you to vent and let go of anger.

5. *Get rid of old projects.* We all have old projects or hobbies we were enthusiastic about years ago that we haven't continued or completed. Now we may feel guilty about the cost involved, so we keep the materials, thinking we'll get back to the project someday. Give these things away to a thrift store or toss them out. Then that project can never bug you again. You can even check it off of your to-do list!

Faithful simplicity means making more room for relationships, for relaxation, and for better spiritual, mental, and physical health. How and what to simplify in our lives is an individual choice. But any attempt at faithful simplicity must begin by imitating Jesus's example and spending some time each day in prayer and quiet with our God.

(Adapted from Susan K. Rowland, "Faithful Simplicity," *Catholic Update*, July 2012.)

Questions for Reflection and Discussion

"Our life is frittered away by detail…. Simplify, simplify!" said Henry David Thoreau.[7] Which of your possessions would you find it hardest to live without?

_____

_____

_____

_____

What does Jesus's radical call to simplicity (Matthew 6:25–34) mean in your life?

_____

_____

_____

_____

Inspiration From the Saints
Catherine of Siena (1347–1380)
A twin and the twenty-fourth of twenty-five children, Catherine entered the lay Third Order of St. Dominic. She was known for her severe disciplines but also for her profound spirituality. After a time of giving herself to contemplation, she came to realize that she must also actively serve others. She carried on extensive correspondence with all kinds of people, from popes and kings to humble workers and even prostitutes. Her theological writings, rooted in deep pastoral experience and common sense, earned her the title of Doctor of the Church. She is one of only four women to be so honored (the others are Teresa of Avila, Thérèse of Lisieux, and Hildegard of Bingen).

Catherine's gift to the Church today is her skill of conciliation among diverse groups. How can your Lenten practice of fasting make you more willing to understand other perspectives?

_____

_____

_____

_____

Practice

The truly mystical Gospel story of the Samaritan woman at the well was already used by the early Church in preparation of the new candidates for baptism on Holy Saturday. All the elements of invitation, disclosure, unfolding levels of meaning, intimacy, reciprocity, and enlightenment are here for the taking. The whole point of the story of the woman at the well is that, unless you experience the Spirit, which Jesus says is "the water that I will give which will turn into a spring within you, welling up unto eternal life" (4:14), the whole thing falls apart.

This week, find one way to simplify your life, a discipline that you can keep practicing once Lent is over.

Prayer

God of all creation, I offer you my all today. Let me practice simplicity at every level of my being in order to live more fully in you. As I empty out the unnecessary things of my life, I seek the fullness of true life and love in you. Give me living water, that I may never thirst. Amen.

Almsgiving

As he walked along, he saw a man blind from birth. His disciples asked him, "Rabbi, who sinned, this man or his parents, that he was born blind?" Jesus answered, "Neither this man nor his parents sinned; he was born blind so that God's works might be revealed in him…. As long as I am in the world, I am the light of the world." When he had said this, he spat on the ground and made mud with the saliva and spread the mud on the man's eyes, saying to him, "Go, wash in the pool of Siloam" (which means Sent). Then he went and washed and came back able to see. The neighbors and those who had seen him before as a beggar began to ask, "Is this not the man who used to sit and beg?"…He kept saying, "I am the man." But they kept asking him, "Then how were your eyes opened?" He answered, "The man called Jesus made mud, spread it on my eyes, and said to me,

'Go to Siloam and wash.' Then I went and washed and received my sight."

—John 9:1–11

Catechism Quote

The works of mercy are charitable actions by which we come to the aid of our neighbor in his spiritual and bodily necessities. Instructing, advising, consoling, comforting are spiritual works of mercy, as are forgiving and bearing wrongs patiently. The corporal works of mercy consist especially in feeding the hungry, sheltering the homeless, clothing the naked, visiting the sick and imprisoned, and burying the dead. Among all these, giving alms to the poor is one of the chief witnesses to fraternal charity: it is also a work of justice pleasing to God.[8]

—CCC, 2447

Who are the hungry, the homeless, the naked, the sick, and the imprisoned in your life? How can you be a better neighbor to them?

_____

_____

_____

_____

What Is Almsgiving?

To many people, giving alms is synonymous with charity. While this is not an incorrect concept, charitable giving is only a small aspect of what we are called to do through the practice of almsgiving. It is a sign of our care for those in need and an expression of our gratitude for all God has given to us. Works of charity and the promotion of justice are integral elements of the Christian way of life we began when we were baptized.

Almsgiving is a natural expression of love extended out to our neighbor. It is a response to what St. Paul notes in 1 Corinthians 13:3, "If I give away all my possessions, and if I hand over my

body so that I may boast, but do not have love, I gain nothing."
It is not empty giving, out of obligation or duty, but an all-encompassing practice that comes from our discipleship.

Perhaps most importantly, almsgiving is part of Christian stewardship, the roots of which are found in Matthew 25:31–46. In our Church today, few concepts are more misunderstood than the concept of Catholic stewardship. Many people hear the word *stewardship* and immediately think "fundraising." But that is not really what stewardship is about.

Good Stewardship

Quite simply, the good steward is the person who takes care of whatever it is that she or he has been entrusted with, and uses it to good purpose. As the U.S. Catholic bishops said in *Stewardship: A Disciple's Response*: "A Christian steward is one who receives God's gifts gratefully, cherishes and tends them in a responsible and accountable manner, shares them in justice and love with others and returns them with increase to the Lord."

Good stewardship affects every part of our lives. If we waste a talent, fritter our time away with worthless pursuits, or squander our resources, something inside of us just doesn't feel right.

That's because our inner compass senses the right direction, even when we sometimes wander off course.

On the other hand, when we are using our time, our talents and our material resources well, we feel in balance, in tune with God. We realize we have been generously given those gifts and, in turn, we are using them for good purposes.

What are some common qualities that good stewards have in common? Successful stewards:

1. *Give until it feels good.* There is something deep within us that is good and generous, some almost biological sensation that is triggered when we see a need. It is that good feeling that wells up within us when another person's needs and our shared gifts intersect. "It is better to give than to receive" might seem like so many lofty words, but as we look back on our lives, we find they are absolutely true. How many times have we found ourselves saying, after we have extended ourselves (even when a bit begrudgingly): I like doing this. Giving feels great; I'm not depleted at all. In fact, I'm enriched! Good stewards capitalize on such moments.

2. *Don't see obligation, but opportunity.* The good steward is awake, alert to opportunities about them, actually looking for chances to make that difference. But note: The good steward is a conscious steward, not a guilty steward. Successful Catholic stewards are not hand-wringing worrywarts: "Am I doing enough? Did I spend enough time there? Did I use my talents to the fullest? Am I as generous as I should be?" Nothing is more corrosive to a good, healthy spirit of stewardship than to be constantly second-guessing yourself. That isn't the way God works with and through us. The good steward joins in God's own generous nature by quite simply and directly addressing the needs of the moment.

3. *Give to specific opportunities.* Good stewards are eager to hear the stories, the modern day parables of lives changed, enriched, made better and more human because of their generosity. They understand that good stewardship is not lived by merely dumping their time, talent, and treasure into some dark hole, while piously folding their hands, eyes cast heavenward, uttering, "I gave." Good stewards, carefully marshaling their

gifts, are willing to be generous, but in turn expect accountability for those gifts they have shared.

Good stewards want to know they helped paint these walls or put on a roof or pay a decent salary to a teacher. It is not that every hour, expression of talent, or dollar must be specifically targeted and then directly attributed to the giver. But there is a real satisfaction, a deserved satisfaction, in knowing that because of their efforts a young mother was provided a safe home for her baby and herself, the youth mission trip went smoothly, the RCIA program is deepening people's faith, or dinners and visits to the widower made an enormous difference after the death of his beloved life's companion.

4. *Have an attitude of gratitude.* Good stewards are constantly aware and amazed by what they have been given. "How lucky I am!" easily comes off their lips and is radiated in their faces. And why not? Each of us has a measure of years that has been allotted to us, a unique combination of abilities showered upon us, and often enough, the material wealth or possessions to supply what we might need or want.

Good stewards have good memories, recalling where they came from, the struggles of their parents, the struggles of their own lives, those peaks and those valleys that shaped them and brought them to this very moment. And they find themselves deeply grateful. It's an "attitude of gratitude." Good stewards know that they didn't earn their time, talents or treasure. These are truly gifts from a generous God—miraculously and randomly scattered over the human race—who asks only that we also be generous.

5. *Share various gifts at the right times.* Good stewardship is not a calcified formula or a specific recipe: "To four parts time, add two parts talent. Sprinkle three parts treasure over the top and serve." At various times in our lives, we will be more able to give of our time, our talents, our treasure. The busy young executive may not have the time to sit in a retirement home and play bingo every morning, but she may have the organizational skills to put that ministry together. A retired couple with a fixed income may have to be careful with their limited resources, but they may be able to spend time in a day-care center with children of working parents.

The good steward practices this truism, "Do what you can, not what you can't." Different situations in the life of our families, our parishes, our communities will call forth different applications of those three trusty pillars of stewardship: time, talent, treasure.

6. *Realize God will point the way.* Stewardship is in our hearts, but like any other discipline, good stewardship takes time to infuse our total being. And so the operative word that the good steward uses is: "Relax!" God is with us on this journey and will show us the way. It is not so much that good stewardship has a learning curve; it is more an experiential curve. In other words as we "do" or live good stewardship, we become better and better at it. And, as we experience that satisfaction (it is really God's grace streaming into our lives) that comes from sharing some portion of our time, our talents and our treasure, we hunger for more. It becomes easier, more natural.

Once a person actively commits herself or himself to the first step—becoming a conscious or intentional steward—the next steps and portions of the stewardship journey will reveal themselves. In people they meet, situations they see, words they hear, they will begin to hear the soft, gentle call of God, asking them to respond.

7. *See stewardship as a spiritual act.* If you think about it for a minute, the realization sets in: God doesn't actually need us to return anything to him. It's all his anyway. First, God gives us life—time. Then he provides the various physical and psychological components, DNA, education, and temperament that create and shape our various talents. Finally, without the application of those talents and abilities over a period of time, there would be no treasure for us to even consider. It is we who need to return some portion of time, talent and treasure as an act of love, of appreciation, of acknowledgment.

Good stewards see this love relationship as a spiritual act. It's an offering to God that in some small but real way mirrors Christ's own life—and a way to return the Father's great love. As good stewardship is a beautifully spiritual act, it is also dangerously contagious. When we see people in our parish leading by example of good stewardship, of not calling attention to their generosity, we are very likely to become "infected." We surely are affected.

The adage attributed to St. Francis applies here: "Preach the gospel, and use words if necessary." That is how good stewards share this bountiful life with God in Christ--not by mouthing pious words, but by actions that speak to the deepest parts of us. Good stewardship calls out to us all.

(Adapted from Paul Wilkes, "Seven Secrets of Successful Stewards," *Catholic Update,* October 2005.)

Questions for Reflection and Discussion
Dag Hammarskjold, secretary-general of the United Nations, said: "In our era, the road to holiness necessarily passes through the way of action."[9] Where is the principle of stewardship most active in your life right now?

_____

_____

_____

_____

What aspect of stewardship—time, talent, or treasure—is most
difficult for you to share? Why?

_____

_____

_____

_____

Inspiration From the Saints
Mother Teresa of Calcutta (1910–1997)

Born in Albania, Teresa joined a religious order and served in India. While acting as principal of a Catholic high school in Calcutta, she was moved by the presence of the sick and dying on the city streets. In 1948 she received permission to leave her post and begin a ministry among the sick, a ministry that led to her founding a new order, the Missionaries of Charity. She received the Nobel Peace Prize in 1979. While not formally canonized, at her death in 1997 the world knew it had lost a saint.

Teresa's special love and care for "the poorest of the poor" make her a special saint for our times. How does your practice of charity and almsgiving help the poor among us?

_____

_____

_____

_____

Practice

This Sunday's Gospel revolves entirely around the theme of light and seeing things truthfully. This problem is at the heart of what almost all ancients saw as the "tragic sense of life." Because humans cannot see their own truth very well, they do not read reality very well either. We all have our tragic flaws and blind spots. Humans always need more "light" or enlightenment about themselves and about the endless mystery of God.

Seek out and follow an as yet unexplored truth in your life this week. Look for places where you can be a light to others.

Prayer

God of all creation, I want to be like you in generous love. Let my actions come from my love of you, and be guided by the work of Jesus, who gave freely of all that he was and possessed, his unending wealth of prayer and presence. Shine your gentle light into the lives of all whose pathways are dark today. Amen.

Conversion

When Mary came where Jesus was and saw him, she knelt at his feet and said to him, "Lord, if you had been here, my brother would not have died." When Jesus saw her weeping, he was greatly disturbed in spirit and deeply moved. He said, "Where have you laid him?" They said to him, "Lord, come and see." Jesus began to weep. So the Jews said, "See how he loved him!"…

Then Jesus, again greatly disturbed, came to the tomb. It was a cave, and a stone was lying against it. Jesus said, "Take away the stone." …So they took away the stone. And Jesus looked upward and said, "Father, I thank you for having heard me. I knew that you always hear me, but I have said this for the sake of the crowd standing here, so that they may believe that you sent me." When he had said this, he cried with a loud voice, "Lazarus, come out!" The dead man came out, his hands and feet

bound with strips of cloth, and his face wrapped in a
cloth. Jesus said to them, "Unbind him, and let him go."

—John 11:32–39, 41–44

Catechism Quote

Christ's call to conversion continues to resound in
the lives of Christians. This second conversion is an
uninterrupted task for the whole Church who, "clasping
sinners to her bosom, [is] at once holy and always in
need of purification, [and] follows constantly the path
of penance and renewal." This endeavor of conversion is
not just a human work. It is the movement of a "contrite
heart," drawn and moved by grace to respond to the
merciful love of God who loved us first.[10]

—CCC, 1428

When did you first recognize a call to change your life to reflect your faith? When did you last recognize this?

_____

_____

_____

_____

The Constant Call to Conversion

As we noted in week one, Lent is about the process of conversion. We turn away from sin and turn to the good news of Jesus Christ. Through our baptism we are born, over and over, again and again. Over and over God rolls back stones from our tombs of complacency, calling us out into the light of life.

Unexpected events—whether heart-lifting or heart-breaking—often nudge us toward questioning the meaning of life. A baby is born. Someone betrays us. We lose a job. We find a friend. News of war and conflict around the world appalls us. We celebrate an anniversary. A relationship ends. A child leaves home. A spouse dies.

In happy times, we ask, "How did we deserve this?" If our answer is, "We don't. It's pure gift. It's pure grace," then we have seen the revelation of God's generous love. In painful times, we ask, "How did we deserve this?" If our answer is, "We don't. And we can't handle this alone," if we turn to God (or to companions as the enfleshment of God) for hope and healing, once again we have tasted the revelation of God's love.

Such times can be conversion times. These moments of revelation are God's call, God's reaching out to us: Conversion and faith are our response.

The Catholic understanding of conversion is not a once-for-all leap into faith: We tend to crawl. We're familiar with Paul's sudden conversion on the road to Damascus, that "born again" experience identified by time and place, and the Holy Spirit can and does sometimes work in such dramatic ways. However, most of our lifelong conversion comes through the Spirit's more subtle action enfleshed in persons and events. Jesus reveals this Spirit of God's love to us in what he says but more by who he is and what he does: healing the sick, forgiving and eating with sinners, caring for the poor, dying and rising. He is the Word made flesh by the power of God's Spirit.

Conversion also has its "plateaus"—the experience of a long, hot day after setting out on our path. Abraham and Sarah did not face crises every day in the desert. They were simply called to live each day in fidelity. Not all of us are able to point to vivid born-again experiences prompted by crises. But we know whether we're living more deeply in God's love today than we did five years ago.

The sacraments and liturgical year help to celebrate and nourish these new conversions. The ordinary is born again into the extraordinary; our faith helps us see this. Eating, drinking, bathing, anointing, reconciling, healing, leading, marrying, using bread, wine, water, oil, gesture and vesture, music, laying on of hands, and taking part in processions in a community of faith— all these human events are caught up into the new creation. Sunday after Sunday, Lent after Lent, year after year, we bring all this to liturgy so that all of life and all creation might be born again and again through God's Spirit who makes all creation new.

Conversion as Dying and Rising

Another image of conversion is the paschal mystery, our entering into the dying and rising of Jesus. This image is grounded in the Rite of Christian Initiation of Adults (RCIA). There the Church offers a vision of conversion for not only for new members, but for all Catholics. "The whole initiation must bear a markedly paschal character, since the initiation of Christians is the first sacramental sharing in Christ's dying and rising." Initiation is the first sharing in Christ's dying and rising; but every sacrament, especially the Eucharist, celebrates our deepening experience of the death and resurrection of Christ.

We need to connect this dying and rising with concrete events in our lives. The writings of the Bible are rooted in historical events and stories—stories of real people to whom God gives life even when they are dead, powerless, or enslaved: to Abraham and Sarah when they are old and barren, to Moses when he is fearful and timid, to the Hebrews in slavery, to Isaiah when he sees himself as too sinful, to Mary who is a virgin, sons and daughters who are prodigal, sheep who are lost, tax collectors who are traitorous, to Jesus tempted in the desert and nailed to the cross. In each story there is death—powerlessness, barrenness, rejection, crucifixion. In each story God gives life—power, birth, acceptance, resurrection.

We proclaim these stories, and we listen. It is not so much that we take hold of the stories but the stories take hold of us. We ask, "Have I ever felt too old, barren, fearful, enslaved, weak, exiled, young, sinful, excluded, prodigal, lost, in a desert or on a cross? If so, do I believe God is there in those times turning to me and offering love, grace, freedom, liberation, gift, life? Have I put my trust in that God, turned to that God? This is surrender of our whole person to the God who surrenders in love to us.

For many people, dying often means a crisis. Dying, however, can also mean the day-to-day dying of people who love, for example, in marriage, friendship, or serving others. In Italian, *amore* (love) has its roots in *morte* (death). In the quiet dailiness of our relationships and our vocations we experience death to self and to our needs. This kind of dying is part of one's care, compassion, sensitivity, and love for others. We experience the new life which death brings—the life for which we give thanks at Eucharist and which is the place of ongoing conversion.

Conversion in the RCIA

There is no better way to understand the meaning of conversion in all its dimensions than to look at the RCIA. This is the Church's own vision for nourishing the ongoing conversion of its members. In the first period of the RCIA (inquiry), a time when candidates for initiation search for faith with the Catholic Christian community, the goal is "faith and initial conversion." Very simply, that means a person "feels called away from sin and drawn into the mystery of God's love."

That may or may not have happened for an inquirer. If it has not, the inquiry period offers evangelization, which means "sharing the Good News" of God's love as an invitation to conversion. We simply tell the great stories of God offering life where there is death. We invite inquirers to see themselves in those stories. "Yes, I am the prodigal embraced by the Father. I am the lost sheep carried home. We are the people with whom Jesus is present during the storm." If we see ourselves in these stories, conversion has happened.

The same is true for baptized Catholics who may or may not have been "drawn into the mystery of God's love. If any of us as baptized Catholics have not experienced personal faith and conversion, we have some catch-up work to do.

The second period in the RCIA, the catechumenate (the period when the Church nurtures candidates in deeper faith), does not totally shift gears. It simply continues what the inquiry period began, and nourishes, stabilizes and deepens the ongoing conversion of new members. It does so in four ways:

1. *Scripture and doctrine.* At the heart of all the great stories of Scripture is God's love calling us through death to life. Do we connect those stories with our own born-again and death-resurrection stories?

2. *Prayer and moral life of the community.* God's love comes first, and makes our love possible. A second sign of conversion for new and old members is that we are praying and living better.

3. *Liturgy.* A third sign of conversion is discovering and celebrating God's presence and love in the liturgy: in bathing, anointing, eating, drinking, reconciling, marrying, leading and healing, in gesture and vesture, smells and bells. The Catholic vision that celebrates God's creation and love in the Eucharist

and other sacraments extends to the whole of creation, rejoicing in God's goodness revealed in all the earth's blessings.

4. *Apostolic witness.* All the baptized are called to Christian witness and service; all are called to be missionaries—especially in their family, work, neighborhoods and civic communities. If we aren't ready to witness actively to the gospel, then we aren't ready for baptism. That means that some of us baptized as infants and raised on a passive diet of "pay, pray, and obey" may yet have a long way to go in activating our missionary vocation.

The Catholic understanding of conversion, therefore, is that we are born again and again, through dying and rising again and again. Conversion is the ongoing response of our whole person turning in faith in the amazing grace of God's love, our response of love in prayer and moral action, celebrating that love in a myriad of liturgies, and witnessing to that love and justice in our world.

(Adapted from Rev. James B. Dunning, "Conversion: Being Born Again and Again and Again," *Catholic Update,* April 1988.)

Questions for Reflection and Discussion

"Each person's task in life is to become an increasingly better person," wrote Leo Tolstoy.[11] What are some of the peak experiences in your life that were also times of conversion?

_____

_____

_____

_____

How has your understanding and experience of conversion changed over these past few weeks of Lent?

_____

_____

_____

_____

Inspiration From the Saints
Francis of Assisi (1182–1226)

Raised in a merchant family, Francis, as a youth, aspired to wealth and military fame. After turning his life over to God, the "little poor man" went through the world full of joy and the love of Jesus. He strove in all things to be an instrument of God's peace. He did this because he saw in every human being as well as in all of creation, not an enemy, but a brother and sister in Christ. Pope John Paul II named St. Francis the patron of ecology in 1979.

Francis's love and respect for all of creation, as well as his example as peacemaker, are qualities that are essential to Christian practice today. How does an appreciation of the natural world inspire you to a deeper experience of conversion?

_____

_____

_____

_____

Practice

In a brilliant finale to the Lazarus story, Jesus invites the onlookers to join him in making resurrection happen: "Move the stone away!... Unbind him, and let him go free!" We must unbind one another from our fears and doubts about the last enemy, death. We must now "see that the world is bathed in light" and allow others to enjoy the same seeing—through our lived life. The stone to be moved is always our fear of death, the finality of death, any blindness that keeps us from seeing that death is merely a part of the Larger Mystery called Life. It does not have the final word.

This week, unbind someone whom you have held bound in unforgiveness. Seek reconciliation with that person, letting God's peace guide your efforts.

Prayer

Again and again, I begin my life anew, God of all creation. Create in me a new heart, and wash away my sins. "You desire truth in the inward being; therefore teach me wisdom in my secret heart" (Psalm 51:6). Your Word, O God, is truth and life. Amen.

Discipleship

Now the eleven disciples went to Galilee, to the mountain to which Jesus had directed them. When they saw him, they worshiped him; but some doubted. And Jesus came and said to them, "All authority in heaven and on earth has been given to me. Go therefore and make disciples of all nations, baptizing them in the name of the Father and of the Son and of the Holy Spirit, and teaching them to obey everything that I have commanded you. And remember, I am with you always, to the end of the age."

—Matthew 28:14–20

Catechism Quote

At last Jesus' hour arrives: he commends his spirit into the Father's hands at the very moment when by his death he conquers death, so that, "raised from the dead by the glory of the Father," he might immediately *give* the Holy

Spirit by "breathing" on his disciples. From this hour onward, the mission of Christ and the Spirit becomes the mission of the Church: "As the Father has sent me, even so I send you."[12]

—CCC, 730

How are you being called by Christ to continue his work?

_____

_____

_____

_____

What Is Discipleship?

What does it mean to be a disciple of Jesus Christ? The gift of our faith is not something we are to hoard for our own benefit; it is meant to be shared with the world. Lent is a good time to wonder about what makes us Catholic, and the particular ways we can follow Christ's call to "Go therefore and make disciples of all nations." In revisiting the deep roots of our faith, we can find the beautiful truths, moral convictions, and spiritual treasury that constitute Catholicism. These will always be powerfully life-giving for us and for the world. Jesus explained to the Samaritan woman, and to disciples ever after, that he had come with "living waters" (read John 4:4–42). At this time, surely, we need to drink deeply from the great refreshing river that is Catholic Christian faith—at its best.

The heart of Christian faith is not the Bible, nor the sacraments, nor the creeds, nor the Church but "a Person, the Person of Jesus of Nazareth, the only Son of the Father" (CCC, 426). By baptism, the fundamental and common vocation of all Christians is to become disciples of Jesus Christ—people who follow "the way" that he modeled and made more possible by his living, dying, and rising.

Catholic Discipleship

The Church offers some distinctive ways to embrace our call to discipleship. Here are nine signal aspects of our faith that can help direct our efforts to follow Christ and bring him to all those in our world:

1. *Positive understanding of the person.* Catholicism insists that the human person is essentially good, ever more graced than sinful. Indeed, we are capable of dreadful sin and destruction, but this is not what first defines us. When the radical Reformers insisted that the human condition is totally corrupt (Calvin more than Luther), the Catholic Church, at the Council of Trent (1545–1563), rejoined that the divine image was never lost to us, even in the "Fall" of Adam and Eve. That all people reflect the image and likeness of God is also the basis of Catholic teachings on the dignity of every person, on the value of human life—from womb to tomb—and that all have the same basic human rights and responsibilities.

2. *Committed to community.* Catholics take Church seriously because we're convinced that both our personhood and Christian faith are inherently communal. Catholicism has consistently taught that God creates us as communal beings, making us responsible for and to each other—even beyond the grave. Death is no barrier to our care for each other. Because the bond of baptism is never broken, we can pray to the saints and for the souls. This communal emphasis of Catholicism is also

the foundation of its social ethic that emphasizes every citizen's responsibility to the common good of the whole society. We must care for the common well-being as well as for our own.

3. *Sacramental outlook.* Catholic faith sees all of God's creation as essentially good. Catholicism has never condemned dancing, singing, celebrating, good food, or alcohol. Yes, everything can be abused but all is first a gift (*gratia*) of God. Similarly, we can embrace our own lives in the world as meaningful and worthwhile, not because of our efforts but by the grace of God.

This graciousness of life in the world finds its high point in the sacramental principle that is so core to Catholic faith. This begins with the conviction that God reaches out to us and we respond through the ordinary and everyday of life, through the created order, through our relationships, through all our good efforts and the experiences that come our way. Climaxed by the seven great sacraments that we celebrate in Church, the sacramental principle encourages Catholics "to see God in all things" (St. Ignatius of Loyola).

4. *Catholics cherish Scripture and Tradition.* Some Protestants believe that scripture alone is the source of God's revelation, and

the Council of Trent reaffirmed the centrality of sacred Scripture as "the norm of norms" for Christian faith. But it reiterated that Christian Tradition, representing the time-tested truths that emerge over the Church's history, is also a "fountain" of divine revelation. This was Catholicism's way of insisting that the Holy Spirit is ever present with the Church, helping to deepen our understanding and to address new questions and circumstances with the wisdom of Christian faith.

5. *Catholics embrace holistic faith.* Jesus preached the great commandment of love as requiring one's whole person—all one's mind, heart, and strength. That old *Baltimore Catechism* answer to "Why did God make you?" reflected such a holistic sense of Christian faith: "to know, love, and serve" God in this life and be happy forever in the next. Christian faith demands our whole being—head, heart, and hands. There is no aspect of our lives from which our faith can be excluded. It should permeate every nook and cranny, on Mondays as well as Sundays. Likewise, faith should be exercised on every level of existence—the personal, interpersonal, and political. Christians should live as disciples of Jesus in every circumstance.

6. *Commitment to justice*. Modern Scripture scholars agree that the central theme in the preaching of Jesus was the coming of God's reign. In keeping with his Jewish faith, Jesus understood God's reign as both personal and social, spiritual and political, for here and hereafter. It calls people to do God's will "on earth as in heaven."

Catholicism has always emphasized that Christian faith demands care for the neighbor in need. But toward the end of the nineteenth century, the Church began to teach explicitly that our faith requires us to work for social justice. Christian faith demands that disciples oppose unjust social structures and work to ensure justice for all. And more than the blind "lady justice" weighing the scales in precise measure, giving everyone no more than their due (Aristotle), the biblical and Catholic sense of justice has a largesse to it. Like their God, God's people should side with the poor and oppressed, favoring those to whom justice is denied.

7. *Universal spirituality*. Spirituality is surely one of the buzzwords of our time; even people who disavow religion will readily claim to be "spiritual." Catholicism's greatest asset may

well be its spirituality and the extraordinary variety of spiritual charisms that mark its life. It is in stark contrast to much of what passes for "new age" spirituality—a warm, fuzzy feeling about a very private relationship with the divine. Catholic spirituality can be summarized as "putting faith to work"—allowing Christian faith to permeate every aspect of daily life. It is sustained by our active membership in a Christian faith community and through disciplines of prayer, worship and conversation. It bears the fruits of compassion, justice and peace for ourselves and for the world.

8. *Catholics are "catholic."* We like to say that catholic means "universal," and indeed it does. That was Aristotle's favored meaning of the word. Its roots are the Greek *katha holos*, which literally mean, "to include everyone." This was likely why early Christian authors like St. Augustine began to use it to describe the Christian community. However, James Joyce may have said it best in *Finnegan's Wake*: "catholic means 'here comes everybody.'"

To be catholic calls a community to welcome all people, regardless of their human circumstances. It demands that we reach out with love for everyone, neighbors next door and on the far side of the world—to care without borders. It requires that we respect people with religions that are different from ours, being open to dialogue and learning from them. And St. Augustine's favored use of *catholic* was "to be open to the truth, wherever it can be found." Parochialism and closed-mindedness are against the Catholic faith.

9. *Devotion to Mary*. Since the beginning of the Church, Mary has held pride of place in the communion of saints. A great debate arose in the early Church about whether or not Mary could have the title "Mother of God." Some said she did not deserve it, being the mother only of the human Jesus. But the faith of the common people insisted that she had borne in her womb this person who was God among us as one of ourselves, and so should be called "Mother of God."

They won the day. Yet, our turning to Mary is also based on a very human instinct. We remember how she interceded with Jesus at the wedding feast of Cana; though he didn't feel ready to launch his public ministry, he honored the request of his mother. Surely for a good son, this pattern continues in eternity. If Mother Mary intercedes for us, how can Jesus decline?

Pope John Paul II repeatedly called Catholics to ask forgiveness for the many ways and times that we have failed to live up to our faith. We must lament and repent that the core convictions outlined above have often been more honored in the breach than the observance. Yet, woven together, they ever challenge us with the great life-giving vision that is Catholic faith. There is no more worthy way to live than with those beautiful truths and values that make us Catholic.

(Adapted from Thomas H. Groome, "Nine Things That Make Us Catholic," *Catholic Update,* September 2004.)

Questions for Reflection and Discussion

What aspect of Catholicism do you most love? What do you find most troubling?

_____

_____

_____

_____

How does being Catholic set you apart—or not—in this world?

_____

_____

_____

_____

Inspiration From the Saints
Blessed Pope John XXIII (1881–1963)

While not formally canonized, the holiness of "good Pope John" is universally recognized. Of poor peasant background, he became a professor of Church history before assuming diverse tasks of Vatican diplomacy. Known for his human warmth and humor and a heart that embraced all peoples, his concern for social justice and for peace on earth came to expression in his encyclicals.

John's confidence in the Spirit, evidenced by his calling the Second Vatican Council, made him a symbol of modern Catholicism. He was truly an ambassador of the faith. How does your practice of the faith make it more inviting to others?

_____

_____

_____

_____

Practice

Jesus is set as the human blueprint, the standard in the sky, the oh-so-hopeful pattern of divine transformation. Who would have presumed that the way to life could be the way of dying? It is, as Paul says, "the secret mystery." This leaves humanity in solidarity with the life cycle, but also with one another, with no need to create success stories for itself, or to create failure stories for others. Humanity in Jesus is free to be human and soulful instead of any false climbing into "Spirit." This was supposed to change everything, and it still will.

Consider your call to be a disciple. How can you best live this out in the year to come? Reflect on what you have learned during this Lenten study, and how it will influence your decision.

Prayer

God of all creation, we come to the end of our Lenten study. As we go forward into the Triduum and the glorious Easter season, let us do so with a renewed mind and heart, eager to experience your redeeming presence in all people and in all things. You are the God of everlasting life. Amen.

Notes

1. *Catechism of the Catholic Church* (Washington, D.C.: USCCB, 1994), 1969, referencing Matthew 6:1–6, 16–18; 6:9–13; Luke 11:2–4.
2. *CCC*, 1430, citing Joel 2:12–13; Isaiah 1:16–17; Matthew 6:1–6, 16–18.
3. Constitution on the Sacred Liturgy, 110.
4. Constitution on the Sacred Liturgy, 110.
5. *CCC*, 2041, 2043, referencing CIC, can. 1246; CCEO, cann. 881, #1, #4; 880, #3.
6. Constitution on the Sacred Liturgy, 110.
7. Henry David Thoreau, quoted in *Simplify, Simplify and Other Quotations from Henry David Thoreau*, K.P. Van Anglen, ed. (New York: Columbia University Press, 1996).
8. *CCC*, 2447, referencing Matthew 25:31–46; Tobit 4:5–11; Sirach 17:22; Matthew 6:2–4.
9. Dag Hammarskjold, *Markings* (New York: Vintage, 2006), p. 103.
10. *CCC*, 1428, referencing *Lumen Gentium*, 8; Psalm 51:17; cf. John 6:44; 12:32; 1 John 4:10.

11. Leo Tolstoy, *Path of Life*. Maureen Cote, trans. (New York: Novinka, 2003), p. 189.

12. *CCC*, 730, referencing John 13:1, 17:1; Luke 23:46; John 19:30; Romans 6:4; John 20:22; John 20:21; Matthew 28:19; Luke 24:47–48; Acts 1:8.

Sources

Dunning, James B. "Conversion: Being Born Again and Again and Again," *Catholic Update*, April 1988.

Groome, Thomas. "Nine Things That Make Us Catholic," *Catholic Update*, September 2004.

Guinan, Michael D. "Christian Spirituality: Many Styles, One Spirit," *Catholic Update*, May 1998.

———. "Saints: Holy and Human," *Catholic Update*, October 1998.

———. "In the Desert With Jesus: Biblical Themes of Lent," *Catholic Update*, February 2005.

Mick, Lawrence E. "Lenten Customs: Baptism Is the Key," *Catholic Update*, March 2003.

Rohr, Richard. *Wondrous Encounters: Scripture for Lent* (Cincinnati: St. Anthony Messenger Press, 2010).

Rowland, Susan K. "Faithful Simplicity," *Catholic Update*, July 2012.

Wilkes, Paul. "Seven Secrets of Successful Stewards," *Catholic Update*, October 2005.

Zagano, Phyllis. "Examen of Consciousness: Finding God in All Things," *Catholic Update*, March 2003.